Excuse Me, Can You Repeat That?

How to Communicate in the U.S.
as an International Student
A Reference Guide

BY
CATHRYN CUSHNER EDELSTEIN

Excuse Me, Can You Repeat That?

How to Communicate in the U.S.
as an International Student
A Reference Guide

BY

CATHRYN CUSHNER EDELSTEIN

Chandler, Arizona

Linda F. Radke, President
Five Star Publications, Inc.
P.O. Box 6698
Chandler, AZ 85246-6698
(480) 940-8182
www.FiveStarPublications.com

www.ExcuseMeCanYouRepeatThat.com

Publisher's Cataloging-in-Publication Data

Edelstein, Cathryn Cushner.
   Excuse me, can you repeat that? : how to communicate in the U.S. as an international student : a reference guide / by Cathryn Cushner Edelstein.

   p. : ill. ; cm.

   Issued also as an ebook.
   Includes bibliographical references.
   ISBN: 978-1-58985-256-3 (pbk.)

   1. Students, Foreign--United States--Handbooks, manuals, etc. 2. Student adjustment--United States--Handbooks, manuals, etc. 3. Cross-cultural orientation--United States--Handbooks, manuals, etc. I. Title.

LB2376.4 .E34 2012
371.826/91   2012947331

eBook provided by

The eDivision of Five Star Publications, Inc.

Printed in the United States of America

Cover Design: Elizabeth Rosen and Kris Taft Miller
Page Layout: Linda Longmire
Editor: Lynda Exley
Project Managers: Patti Crane and Lisa Baumann

Acknowledgment

I wish to thank many people for inspiring me to write this reference guide. First and foremost, I am grateful to my international students and clients, past and present, for providing me with a wealth of global experiences. They are the reason I wrote this guide. Secondly, I greatly appreciate the support of my family: my parents, Estelle and Richard; my sisters, Susan and Stacey; and my daughters, Alexandra and Carly. In addition, I wish to thank Ivan, a constant source of support and motivation, and my colleagues at Emerson College, especially Dr. Linda Moore and Dr. Janis Andersen.

Introduction

Over the last thirty years, I have been fortunate to work with some very special individuals, people who have come to the United States to either work, study or live here. In their effort to assimilate, some have called upon me to improve their English language skills and familiarity with North American culture. Many have come from collective cultures where behavioral expectations are very different than those in the United States, which has an individualist culture. Some have traveled from countries where although the culture, similar to the United States, is individualist, the manner by which people communicate is entirely different. Cultural differences most definitely affect communication, behavior, and language. As most have learned English in their native countries from a nonnative English speaker, the instruction they received in conversational English has been adequate but not enough to comfortably communicate once they find themselves living in the United States. In addition, very little about North American culture and general rules about communicating in common situations have been included. The result is students can speak basic English, but the clarity of their speech and lack of knowledge about what to say in daily situational dialogues is less than good, leaving them frustrated with their skills.

In this book, I hope to provide readers with insight into how to navigate through communicating in the United States so that language and cultural frustrations are lessened. I have been both a speech consultant and a communication professor—and no matter which my students have been, business professionals or college students, the individuals I have worked with have improved their American English skills and found it easier to communicate.

Communication

Communication can be broken down into two categories: verbal and nonverbal communication. Verbal communication includes all aspects of oral communication, the spoken word, and nonverbal communication relates to body language and inferences of communication made without speaking.

CHAPTER 1

VERBAL COMMUNICATION

You have come or are planning to go to the United States, and now you must put to practice what you have learned in English—grammar, intonation, pronunciation, vocabulary, and intent. You may have spent time preparing to speak in English, but you are nervous to do so. Know that people from the United States are usually patient with people who try to speak English. Don't hesitate to try, because after all, without practice, progress cannot happen. You may always speak English with an accent; that is, your intonation patterns and pronunciation will not be native sounding, but with some easy and manageable techniques, you can speak English with clarity. With this in mind, I will break down verbal communication into categories, providing helpful suggestions to make your ability to communicate verbally in the United States easier. I will provide some insight into common errors that cause the most frustration and offer suggestions to remedy them.

▪ Grammar

As you learned grammar, you were taught how to correctly formulate a sentence with nouns, adjectives, verbs, prepositions, articles, and adverbs. Simple sentences, compound sentences, and complex sentences were taught and practiced with tests, drills, and practice. Past tense, Present tense and Future tense were taught with timelines to show you how and when to use them. Now it's time to put it all together and see if you can express your ideas, needs, and intentions correctly so that others in the United States can understand you. Students and clients alike have been surprised at how easy it has been to use what they learned, but they unintentionally make some common errors. In the following section, I will focus on the two forms of grammatical errors I often hear—articles and plurals.

Articles

Many languages around the globe do not use articles before nouns, but in English we do. Using 'a' as an indefinite article or 'the' as a definite article expresses the specificity of a noun.

-Use 'a' for general reference, if the noun hasn't been discussed before.

-Use 'the' for a specific reference, if you and your listener know which noun you are talking about.

Time and again, I hear international students say something such as, "I came to United States three weeks ago and live in dorm." Although a listener can understand this sentence, the omission of the articles, 'the' and 'a' is noticeable right away and should be attended to when communicating in English. First, 'the United States,' is a geographic location and is always expressed with 'the' in front of it, no matter what. In this instance, if a specific 'dorm' has not been mentioned prior, then the speaker should use 'a' before the word 'dorm.' The correct way to say this sentence is, "I came to the United States three weeks ago and live in a dorm."

Tip:

Geographic locations that are a compilation of places in one greater location always need the article 'the' before it. For example use the determiner 'the' with these countries: the Netherlands, the United Arab Emirates, and the United Kingdom. Also use 'the' with all groups of islands such as, the Caribbean Islands and the Fiji Islands. Mountain ranges such as the Alps and the Himalayas also need the article 'the' before the name. Large areas of lakes such as the Finger Lakes of upstate New York and the Great Lakes, which border the United States and Canada, also need the article 'the.'

Cathryn Cushner Edelstein

Plurals and Non-Count Nouns

If a noun cannot be counted with one, two and so on, its plural doesn't require an /s/ on the end. Let's take the noun 'advice,' one I hear over and over incorrectly pluralized with an /s/. It is a non-count noun and stays as is when used in the singular and plural form. In the sentence, "He gave me good advice." or "He gave me a lot of advice." the word form stays the same.

These are some of the most common words that I hear pluralized incorrectly:

Non-Count Noun	singular	plural
advice	piece of	the, some, a lot of, or no determiner
equipment	piece of	the
mail	piece of	the
fish	piece of	the
grammar		some or no determiner
homework		some, a lot of, or no determiner
man	the, a	men
education	an	some, a lot of, or no determiner
baggage	piece of	the
knowledge		some, a lot of, or no determiner
clothing	piece of	the, some, a lot of
rain	the	the
research		some, a lot of, or no determiner
information	piece of	the, some, a lot of, or no determiner
money		some, a lot of, or no determiner
person	a, the	people
furniture	piece of, the	some, a lot of, or no determiner

When using these or any non-count words, you will need to decide how you want to indicate whether you are using them in the singular or plural context. As seen in the chart on the previous page, in some cases using 'a piece of' as in 'a piece of advice' or 'a piece of information' indicates it is singular. If you desire to use the plural form, you would indicate this by saying 'some advice' or 'advice.'

Examples:

My doctor gave me a piece of advice. He said I should exercise regularly. (singular)

My doctor gave me a lot of advice. He said I should exercise regularly, eat less, and try to avoid fried food. (plural)

▪ Intonation

Intonation is the music of a language. Every language has a particular intonation pattern that it follows, when to rise in pitch or drop down in pitch. For example, when speaking Italian, the pitch flows upwards at the end of phrases. In contrast, many of the native languages of India are spoken monotone. If you speak English but are using the music of your native language, you may have difficulty being understood. When speaking English here in the United States, we follow particular intonation patterns that cue the listener about the meaning of what we are saying. It is not only the words that give meaning to what you are expressing, but the intonation pattern as well that suggests emotion. In some languages, emotion is expressed by volume and in others by tonal quality. American intonation patterns vary depending on whether we are making a statement or asking a question. When making statements, we rise in pitch on important words in a phrase and end with a drop in pitch at the end of each sentence. Questions follow different intonation patterns. I will explain more about asking questions a bit later.

Cathryn Cushner Edelstein

Intonation Patterns - Statements

It is easier to take look at the typical intonation pattern of a statement by using letters to replace words. The first letter, 'a' is spoken at a low pitch, then leap up in pitch on the second letter and gradually drop the pitch with each letter, ending with the letter 'f' at the lowest pitch. The idea is that you elevate your pitch on the important idea in the statement and lower your pitch at the end.

Be careful to rise in pitch up to 'b' and not glide to this letter or just get louder on 'b.'

Try this pattern:

```
          b
        c
          d
  a           e
                f
```

This is correct – each letter has its own pitch level.

You **DON'T** want to do this:

```
      a   b
    a       c
   a          d
  a             e
                 f
```

This is what it looks like to glide up on the letter 'a' to 'b.'

You **DON'T** want to do this:

a **B** c d e f   monotone   (the B represents a loud voicing of this letter.)

Once you feel you have mastered this intonation pattern with letters, try using this pattern with words. The first part of the sentence, containing the pronoun and verb, are said at a lower pitch and the word "not," which is very important in this sentence, is emphasized by a rise in pitch. The rest of the words drop in pitch, one syllable at a time, ending with a low pitch.

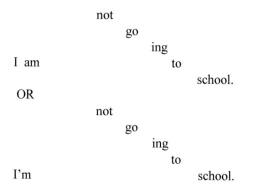

```
                    not
                          go
                                ing
  I  am                            to
                                        school.
     OR
                    not
                          go
                                ing
                                    to
  I'm                                   school.
```

All syllables are separated by a pitch change. By simply using this intonation pattern, your English becomes easier for an American to understand. This is especially important when talking on the phone where nonverbal cues are not given. Listen to a clip of an American news reporter and you will hear this pattern used repeatedly. Reporters use this method to not only clearly articulate the news, but also to keep listeners interested. This pattern promotes listener comprehension, and even with an accent, it will help you to be better understood whenever you speak English.

Cathryn Cushner Edelstein

Intonation Patterns – Questions

As mentioned previously, the pitch pattern changes when asking questions. There are two types of questions: Affirmative/Negative and Informational. Questions that require an affirmative response (yes) or negative response (no) differ in intonation pattern from informational questions. Affirmative/Negative questions begin with Do, Does, Did, Will, Can, Are, and Is start low in pitch and end in higher pitch.

Example:

"Does the train run regularly?" The answer would contain the response, "yes" or "no."

```
                              ly ?
                         lar
                      u
                 reg
              run
        train
      the
Does
```

OR

"Do you like sugar in your tea? Again, the answer would contain the response, "yes" or "no."

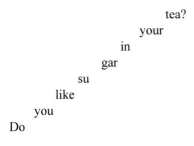

```
                        tea?
                  your
               in
            gar
         su
      like
   you
Do
```

Questions that require answers with informational content are called informational questions and they follow the opposite pattern, starting at a high pitch, and lowering the pitch on each syllable. Questions that begin with, How, When, Why, What, Where, and Who are all considered informational questions.

Example:
"Why are you so happy today?"

```
Why
     are
          you
               so
                    hap
                         py
                            to
                                 day?
```
OR

"What time does the bus leave?"
```
   What
      time
        does
           the
              bus
                leave?
```

Tag questions are a combination of two intonation patterns–a statement and a question:

Example:
"You understand, don't you?"

```
   You
      un
         der                    you?
            stand,
                       don't
```

OR

"He left at noon, didn't he?"

He
    left
       at   he?
          noon,
               didn't

▪ Pronunciation

Students in my classes are most surprised that sounds or phonemes in English are often produced differently from the way they were taught in their native countries. Many were taught to approximate the phonemes; that is, they were not told how to articulate the sounds, but to do so by 'ear'—by listening to a sound and then attempting to make a similar sound. This method works to a point, but to actually pronounce the phonemes correctly in English, there are specific places of articulation – places in the mouth that the tongue must touch. In the following, I will describe the correct placement of articulation for each specific American English phoneme. Each phoneme will be explained using the International Phonetic Alphabet (IPA). It is best to learn the IPA as it breaks down each phoneme and is used in dictionaries and thesauruses throughout the world. To practice, it is best to use a mirror, and watch as your tongue touches the correct place inside your mouth while you follow the instructions. It will feel awkward at first, but if you look around at native speakers of English, you will find that these methods of articulation are used and not viewed as strange. An important thing to remember is that the tongue is a muscle, and it may be difficult to train that muscle to do something different. Also, as with any muscle, the tongue may feel strained while it performs different movements. This is to be expected, but like any muscle that you exercise, it will become easier over time.

Voiced and Voiceless Sounds

Phonemes fall into two categories: voiced and voiceless. Voiced sounds are produced with a voice; that is, your voice is audible because the vocal chords vibrate when making a particular sound. Voiceless sounds on the other hand are produced with a breath of air. You can actually feel the air pass through your lips if you hold your hand up in front of your mouth. While all vowels are voiced sounds, all consonants are not.

Most consonant sounds can best be described in articulation pairs, that is, the exact same place of articulation can produce two different consonant sounds when either voiced or voiceless. In the following sections, this will be described in detail—but this is important information to recognize.

Pronunciation of Vowels

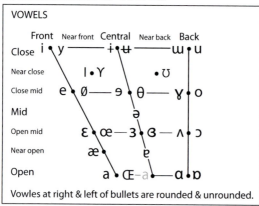

Diagram: Nohat Grendelkhan via Wikimedia Commons

Vowles at right & left of bullets are rounded & unrounded.

You will notice in the diagram above that there are closed, mid, and open vowels. These define the position of your lips and where the sound is produced inside the mouth. As you practice saying these sounds, be aware that the vowel sounds should resonate or vibrate in the front, center, or back of your mouth.

Practice the front vowels first and remember to keep your tongue down and flat. As you begin, make the shape of a smile with your lips, opening your mouth a bit more with each vowel sound as you progress through these front vowels: /i/ - 'ee' as in bee, /I/ - 'ih' as in pin, /e/ - 'ay' as in bake, / ε / - 'eh' as in bet, /æ/- 'áh' as in bat and /a/ - 'au' as in father. Now try producing the

Cathryn Cushner Edelstein

central vowels with your lips in a relaxed position and your mouth open very slightly: /ə/ (called a 'shwa') - 'uh' as in about, and /ʌ/ - 'uh' as in sun. The back vowels are produced with your lips in a circular shape. As you progress through these sounds, raise the back of your tongue a bit higher with each sound: /ʊ/ as in put and book, /u/ - 'ooh' as in blue, /o/ - 'oh' as in boat, /ɔ/ - 'aw' as in bought, and /ɒ/ - 'ohw' as in wall (/ɒ/ is not a commonly used sound in American English).

Here is a short list of words to practice the vowels sounds:

Front Vowels

/i/	/ɪ/	/e/	/ ɛ /	/æ/	/a/
seat	sin	made	set	sat	father
feet	been	fame	mess	mass	car
week	trip	take	went	bath	aunt
please	pill	train	plenty	black	

Central Vowels

/ə/	/ʌ/
about	under
o'clock	ugly
the	love
afraid	such

Back Vowels

/ʊ/	/o/	/u/	/ɔ/
took	stole	zoo	saw
pull	flow	who	ball
cook	whole	two	call
should	bowl	suit	walk

It gets a bit more complicated when we add consonant sounds to the vowels, but the basic way we produce vowels remains constant—we just add on movements in combination with a voice or breath.

Pronunciation of Consonants

Whether voiced or voiceless, consonant sounds are produced with particular tongue and/or lip movements. The diagram on the next page shows the physical characteristics of the mouth. The points of articulation to produce consonant sounds correctly, involve the hard palate, the soft palate, the alveolar ridge, the lips and teeth (see diagram). By using one's lips, tongue tip, or tongue blade in a particular fashion while producing either a vocal (voiced) sound or a breath sound (voiceless), a consonant is produced. In the following section, I will review the correct way to produce each of the American English consonant phonemes. It is likely that you have learned to produce some correctly and others incorrectly, and this is why others may have trouble understanding you when you speak English. Without correct placement to produce these sounds, the sounds are approximated, and not fully audible. Combining word after word filled with errors in pronunciation confuses a listener and ultimately can frustrate you, the speaker. If you have the opportunity to watch native speakers of English as they speak, pay close attention to how they produce the words they are saying. You will notice that they seem to flow from phoneme to phoneme, word to word, easily. In part, this is because they are producing the sounds with correct articulation, and moving their tongue and lips in such a way that they seamlessly blend one sound with another. You do this naturally in your native language. Of course, as a native of any language, learning a language as an infant is a natural process and thus is done without teaching one the correct way to produce a sound. As a nonnative speaker however, learning how to correctly produce English phonemes will assist in assuring that you speak clearly as you communicate in English.

Cathryn Cushner Edelstein

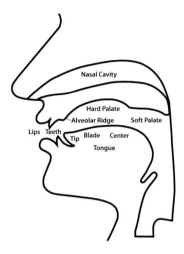

Many languages contain sounds that are not present in English. Likewise, English contains sounds that may not exist in your native language. For example, some Asian languages such as Chinese and Japanese do not contain all of the consonant and vowel sounds that appear in the English language. Most words in these languages do not have final consonant sounds; instead, they end with a vowel or nasal sound. Learning to end a word with a consonant sound may be difficult for people who are not used to doing this. Another example, is in French or Hebrew, you may have trouble with the English pronunciation of /r/ and /h/. In my classes, the /r/, universally, seems to be the one consonant that most students have problems pronouncing correctly in English, no matter what the native language is. Interestingly, it is one sound that seems to vary the most among languages. In English, it is not trilled, does not vibrate and is not formed in the back of the mouth, but rather it is produced in the center of the mouth at an elevated point. Those who are not used to producing English phonemes may find that this guide is teaching you how to produce them properly for the first time. As you review the correct method of producing the American consonant sounds, keep in mind that doing anything new will feel uncomfortable and unnatural at first. Practice the sounds individually as instructed below, and use a mirror if necessary to make sure you are placing your tongue and lips as instructed.

As mentioned before, most consonants come in voiceless and voiced pairs. Simply by placing the tongue in one position and choosing to either vocalize it or give it a breath will produce a different consonant. For example, the consonant phonemes /f/ and /v/ are produced by putting the top front teeth on the bottom lip. Voicing it produces the /v/ sound and giving breath to it produces the /f/ sound.

The following is based on the pronunciation of standard American English. It should be noted, however, that there are of course regional dialects within the United States, just as there are in most countries.

VOICED		VOICELESS	
/b/	**b**uck	/p/	**p**uck
/m/	**m**iss		

Bilabial (both lips touching each other).

The /b/ and /p/ are paired.
The /m/ is produced the same way but has a nasal quality.

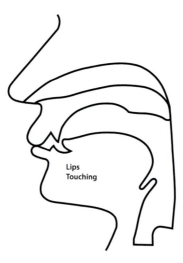

Lips
Touching

Cathryn Cushner Edelstein

VOICED		VOICELESS
/w/	**w**on	

The /w/ is produced with the lips near each other and rounded.

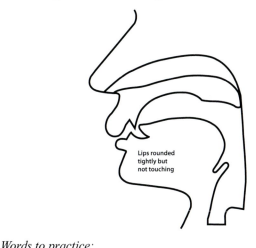

Lips rounded
tightly but
not touching

Words to practice:

/b/	/p/	/m/	/w/
Initial Position			
bit	pit	mit	wit
but	putt	mutt	watt
bill	pill	mill	will
Middle Position			
above	apple	amber	bewilder
stable	staple	ample	away
habit	happy	hummer	awake
Final Position			
cab	cap	ham	how
slab	slap	slam	slow
cub	cap	ram	row

VOICED	VOICELESS
/v/ **very**	/f/ **fun**

Labiodental (lips are touching teeth) /v/ and /f/ are paired.

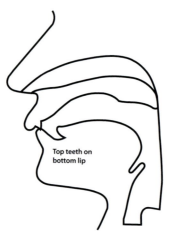

Top teeth on
bottom lip

Words to practice:

/v/	/f/
Initial Position	
vast	fast
vault	fault
verge	forge
Middle Position	
livery	lift
given	offer
oven	after
Final Position	
live	life
love	half
grove	giraffe

VOICED		VOICELESS	
/ð/	this	/θ/	thin

Dental (tongue is placed between upper and lower teeth) /ð/ and /θ/ are paired.

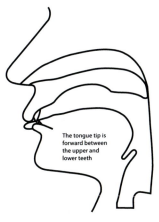

The tongue tip is forward between the upper and lower teeth

Words to practice:

/ð/	/θ/

Initial Position

that	think
there	thank
those	thought

Middle Position

father	bathroom
gather	Athens
either	pathway

Final Position

bathe	bath
breathe	width
clothe	mouth

VOICED		VOICELESS	
/d/	**d**o	/t/	**t**o
/n/	**n**o		
/l/	**l**ow		

Alveolar Ridge (tongue tip touches the alveolar ridge) /d/ and /t/ are paired.

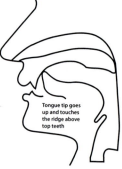

Tongue tip goes up and touches the ridge above top teeth

Words to practice:

/d/	/t/	/n/	/l/
Initial Position			
dab	tab	nab	lab
den	ten	knit	lit
dot	too	new	loop

Middle Position

*double /t/ in the middle of a word sounds like a /d/

butter	sweater	banner	holler
under	fighter	painter	filler
sliding	writing	raining	falling

Final Position

fade	fate	feign	file
grade	great	grain	rail
learned	sight	again	meal

Cathryn Cushner Edelstein

VOICED		VOICELESS	
/z/	**zoo**	/s/	**so**

Alveolar Ridge (tongue blade touches the alveolar ridge) /z/ and /s/ are paired.

The tongue blade is up touching the ridge

Words to practice:

/z/	/s/

Initial Position

/z/	/s/
zeal	seal
zest	simple
zealot	sitter

Middle Position

* It is common for the /s/ followed by a vowel in the middle position to sound like a /z/.

advisor	sister
laser	faster
fuzzy	crystal

Final Position

* It is common for the /s/ followed by an /e/ in the final position to sound like a /z/.
* The /c/ in the final position followed by an /e/ sounds like an /s/.

haze	face
maze	class
pose	place

	VOICED	VOICELESS
/r/	**r**oom	

Hard Palate (tongue tip is pointed at the hard palate but doesn't touch it, while the sides of the tongue are widened, lips are rounded).

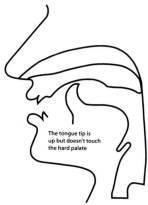

The tongue tip is up but doesn't touch the hard palate

Words to practice:

/r/

Initial Position

run

rate

rack

Middle Position

fairest

market

started

Final Position

mother

gather

joker

Cathryn Cushner Edelstein

VOICED		VOICELESS	
/ʒ/	measure	/ʃ/	**sh**oe

Blade of the tongue is up and back and the sides of the tongue touch the inside of the upper back teeth in these sounds: /ʒ/ and /ʃ/ are paired.

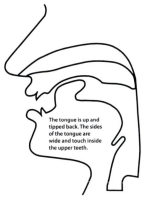

The tongue is up and tipped back. The sides of the tongue are wide and touch inside the upper teeth.

Words to practice:

/ʒ/	/ʃ/
Initial Position	
None	sheet
	shore
	Chicago
Middle Position	
usual	passion
television	creation
confusion	facial
Final Position	
garage	cash
mirage	plush
corsage	trash

VOICED		VOICELESS	
/dʒ/	**just**	/tʃ/	**ch**oice

Blade of the tongue is up and back and the sides of the tongue touch the inside of the upper back teeth while the tongue tip is in the /d/ or /t/ position. /dʒ/ and /tʃ/ are paired.

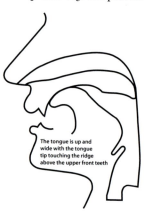

The tongue is up and wide with the tongue tip touching the ridge above the upper front teeth

Words to practice:

/dʒ/	/tʃ/
Initial Position	
Jacob	cheek
judge	chant
jam	chicken
Middle Position	
badger	mischief
pigeon	kitchen
stranger	furniture
Final Position	
average	catch
courage	crunch
change	match

Cathryn Cushner Edelstein

VOICED		VOICELESS	
/g/	**g**o	/k/	**k**ick
/ŋ/	si**ng**		

Back of the tongue is pressed against the soft palate. /g/ and /k/ are paired.

The sound /ŋ/ is produced the same way but has a nasal tone.

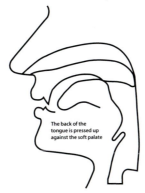

The back of the tongue is pressed up against the soft palate

Words to practice:

/g/	/ŋ/	/k/
Initial Position		
gamble	None	cake
gallop		kind
gobble		castle
Middle Position		
dagger	finger	tinker
foggy	longer	stinky
bigger	anger	tanker
Final Position		
brag	anything	think
frog	sting	plank
drug	playing	stark

VOICED		VOICELESS	
	/h/	**h**ome

This sound is different because it has no place of articulation. It is produced in the back of the mouth/throat with some tension in that area.

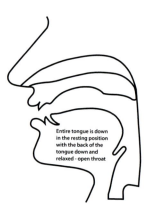

Entire tongue is down in the resting position with the back of the tongue down and relaxed - open throat

Words to practice:

Initial Position
how
hello
happen

Middle Position
forehead
overheard
somehow

Final Position
None

Cathryn Cushner Edelstein

CHAPTER 2

NONVERBAL COMMUNICATION

Every culture has its own rules for nonverbal language, what is appropriate and what is not. Nonverbal language applies to the use of eye contact, facial expression, gesturing with arms and hands, and body movements. Though some aspects of nonverbal communication are universal, most are not. The differences exist because of specific rules of communication that particular cultures hold. For example, nonverbal communication in many cultures has rules for how and when communication can take place between men and women and people of different status. Knowing and understanding the rules of nonverbal communication most often used in the United States will help you when you communicate during your stay here.

▪ Rules of Space/Proximity

In some cultures standing very close to an individual while talking to them indicates that you know the person well or intimately. This is definitely true for people in the United States. Here, people are uncomfortable with a small distance between the speaker and the listener unless they are intimate, close friends, or a relative. In contrast, people from Latin America, for example, often speak loudly during casual conversations and prefer a small distance between speaker and listener, with only one and a half to two feet of space between them. The term, 'proxemics' was created by researcher Edward Hall in the late 1950s. He studied peoples' perceptions of space and distance, including how much space is needed for two people to converse comfortably.

Per Hall, it is very important to understand how one views their own space and territory in order to make someone feel comfortable.

According to Hall, Americans view distance, space, and volume in the following way:

Very Close and Close/Intimate distance: embracing, touching, whispering
0 to 12 inches or 0 to 30.5 cm

Neutral or Personal distance: interactions among close friends, low voice
20 to 36 inches or 50.8 to 91.4 cm

Neutral or Personal distance: public information, full voice
4.5 to 5 feet or 137.2 to 152.4 cm

Across a room or Social distance: speaking to a group, loud voice
8 to 20 feet or 243.8 to 609.6 cm

More than 20 feet or 609.6 cm: loud voice, shouting

Being aware of spatial boundaries when communicating with someone is important because a speaker never wants to unintentionally make their listener feel uncomfortable. How far apart do people stand when speaking causally in your native country? Do they speak quietly or use a loud voice? A person whose personal comfort zone is being compromised may appear uncomfortable and uneasy. They may look troubled, try to back away, or walk away to avoid this feeling. Knowing this, you as a foreign speaker of English can interpret these signs of discomfort and avoid making someone feel uncomfortable altogether by respecting the accepted cultural spatial boundary. This is a natural, instinctual reaction and should not be misinterpreted as thinking the person does not like you—they just need some space.

Nonverbal Signs – showing interest in a person

Many times, students tell me they are unsure of how to read peers' nonverbal language in classrooms. Making new friends can be a challenging experience when many cultures view not only proxemics differently, but eye contact as well. Take notice when you come to the United States as to how far apart people

Cathryn Cushner Edelstein

are when they are talking to you. Use this as a cue to respond the same way. If a classmate is standing near you or pulls his seat up next to you, they are letting you know nonverbally that they may want to interact with you or may want to be available to talk to you at some point. How do you know this? Moving closer in proximity to you, is a nonverbal sign of interest. Likewise, if a fellow student moves away from you, they are nonverbally letting you know they are not interested in communicating with you at that time. Sometimes however, a person may be shy; and although they are not standing or sitting near you, you find them glancing at you several times. This means something entirely different––either they are interested in you, but may be timid and do not know how to approach you, or are simply acknowledging that you are in the room. How can you tell which is the case? If you have eye contact with that person, and they smile at you, they are letting you know that they would probably like to connect with you. At some point, in the future, this may be a person who you can start a conversation with. It is up to you whether you want to begin slowly moving closer to this person, return the smile, or let them take the lead in making a more formal connection with you. If no facial expression, such as a smile is noticed, then they are simply glancing at you. If you don't return the glance with a smile, you are letting the other person know you do not wish to engage with them.

■ Eye Contact

In addition to spatial boundaries, eye contact is very important. Looking at someone directly eye to eye, how long one holds the gaze, or how often he or she looks away, up or down, right or left, will give you feedback about how the person you are talking to is responding to your spoken message. When people from the United States learn to speak, they are taught that looking directly into someone's eyes while speaking and listening is of utmost importance. It symbolizes respect, honesty, confidence, and attentiveness.

Culturally, you may not have the same rules for eye contact during conversation. In Japan, for example, it is considered rude to gaze into someone's eyes during casual conversation for a long while, and in some countries it is considered improper behavior for women to hold eye contact with a man. In the United States, it is good manners to have eye contact with and between both genders. It not does matter the status, rank, or hierarchy of a person. Americans view eye contact as necessary in communication.

Whether you are speaking with a friend, your doctor, professor or supervisor, you should look directly at them while conversing. However, holding a gaze without dialogue can mean something different entirely, usually anger or assertiveness but not always. Staring at someone without talking may cause an intense reaction. The person you are staring at will begin to feel uncomfortable after only a second or two and either stare back at you with a look of confusion or simply turn away from you. It is considered rude to stare at someone for a length of time greater than just a glance unless you know the person and wish to converse with him or her.

If two people are casually discussing a topic, they will look directly at each other throughout the conversation, only looking away briefly. If one person looks down for a long while during the conversation, this could mean they don't agree with what you are saying, that they are uncomfortable with the topic being discussed, or they are thinking deeply about what has just been said. If either of these should happen, you should think about how the person you are talking to is processing what you are saying. It is best to pause in this instance and try to understand why the listener is glancing away from you. You may wish to acknowledge the listener's reaction in this instance and ask them politely what they are thinking.

If the listener looks up during a conversation, it probably means they are bored or disinterested with what you are saying. You may want to consider restating what you are saying to hold your listener's interest. Continuing to talk without acknowledging their reaction will eventually lead to the listener ending the conversation, becoming angry, or possibly walking away from you.

The direction of one's glance can tell a well-trained listener whether you are being truthful or not. Looking left while speaking is usually associated with the belief that the speaker is trying to remember something. Looking right usually denotes creative

Cathryn Cushner Edelstein

thinking or lying. This can be especially important to know when being interviewed. Interviewers are skilled and look for eye contact when evaluating a potential employee or student. You never want to assert that your answer is being fabricated or untrue.

In every culture the different variations of eye contact send a different message. In the United States, you may be told you aren't listening to someone, but in reality you are. Maybe it's because you are not looking at the person while they were speaking. It may seem silly, but in the United States, people often require eye contact to show they are focused on listening. We all know a person can listen to someone while doing an unrelated task, but this lack of eye contact sends a message to the speaker that they are not a priority at that moment and often leaves a speaker frustrated. Whether speaking one on one, sitting in a classroom listening to a teacher or fellow students, or to a speaker at a business meeting, show that you are being attentive and interested by looking directly at the speaker, nodding in agreement with what's been said, or smiling at the speaker.

Now that we have discussed basic eye contact, let's review expressions of emotion one can transfer to another with just the eyes. It is often said that the eyes are the window to a person's soul. If this is true, then the eyes must have the depth and capacity to express many feelings. Some of these expressions are universal, but because in many parts of the world eye contact is prohibited or has different meanings, I will share the most common of them used in the United States.

1. **Surprise/Excitement/Shock** - Raising one's eyebrows while looking at a person, whether they are speaking or not, will signal surprise or excitement. This is often used after a person has shared a story or some information that the listener simply finds shocking or exciting. For example, if a person enters a room and has a dozen freshly baked cookies in a box and gives them to you while saying, "I just baked some cookies today, and I would like to give you some," you would be pleasantly surprised and raise your eyebrows while taking them, saying, "Thank you."

2. Doesn't Understand/Confusion - If one's eyebrows are pulled tightly together while tensing their forehead muscles, this signifies that what has just been heard or seen is not believable or that the person doesn't understand the information just heard. You may use this when you are confused. Or, as a foreign speaker of English, your accent or the grammar you use to say something may trigger this look from a listener. Be sure to know that you are not upsetting the listener, it is just that they are having trouble understanding you. This direct nonverbal feedback from a listener means you should attempt to restate what you just said. Try saying it slower or in a different way. Americans are usually very patient with foreign speakers of English and will wait for you try to make them understand what you want to say.

3. Flirting - If a person looks down at the floor and up to a person's eyes and then down again, this is a flirtatious glance; one that a person will use to show interest in another person. This is done in this manner so that the person will not be seen as aggressive with their flirtation, but instead meek and timid. A more aggressive form of flirtatious eye contact is gazing at someone directly for more than a few seconds or gazing at their entire body from head to toe while smiling. Expressions of flirtation are often seen between people in social situations where interest in another is appropriate to share. Doing this in a place of business or in school is not appropriate and is seen as rude.

4. Lack of Confidence/Shyness - Looking down and away from the gaze of a speaker may signal to a listener that one lacks confidence or is shy. If looking directly at someone while conversing shows confidence, then looking down can be seen as the antithesis. As it is difficult for a person to understand why someone may be looking down and away, the first inclination will be to think they lack confidence. Shyness is usually assumed later as someone's personality is better known. Thus, it is very important that one hold eye contact during conversation—especially during an interview when showing confidence is of utmost importance.

Cathryn Cushner Edelstein

5. Fear - The eyes certainly know how to express fear. This reaction is universal: wincing the eyes, and almost closing them totally shows fear and visceral discomfort with something. Listening to a person who sings off tune, or listening to a dentist's drill often provokes this reaction. Waiting for a scary scene in a movie or waiting for a teacher to hand back a graded exam may also cause one to express this fearful look.

■ Gesturing

One of the more entertaining classes I taught was when several international graduate students and I discussed gesturing. It is amazing how one gesture provokes such different reactions in different places around the world. A very negligible gesture in the United States, crossing the middle and pointer fingers which means 'wish me luck' or 'I hope this comes true' means something totally different in the Vietnam, where this same gesture means two people being intimate with each other. With this as an example, it is best to make sure the meaning of a gesture you are about to use will be understood the way you intend!

Gesturing, or using one's hands and arms and even one's body to express something, is of course cultural. The types of possible gestures people use in the United States are in the hundreds, as is the case where you come from. Gestures are meant to communicate something to another person—whether it is an expression that accompanies speech, or one that is used without speech. With various connotations assigned to gestures around the globe, make sure you use gestures that don't offend others.

Showing the sole of one's shoes in the Middle East and in many Asian countries is considered disrespectful, while in the United States it carries no negativity. Holding two fingers in a 'V,' palm in or out, means 'peace' in the United States. Most Europeans would translate this gesture to mean victory if the palm is facing inward and 'get out of my space' if the palm is facing outward. Nodding your head up and down in the United States tells the person watching that you agree with them or are saying "yes." In Bulgaria and Greece, nodding this way tells a person the opposite, they don't agree or are saying "no." It is best to look on the internet for a complete list of these, as they are too numerous to list in this guide.

Gestures that accompany speech:

How one gestures while speaking is often thought of as being related to one's cultural identity or ethnicity. Many studies have been done to search for commonalities in gesturing among groups of people from specific ethnicities and cultures. Findings indicate that gesturing is indeed cultural in its use. Of course, not all people from a particular culture will use the same gestures, but for the most part they do, or at least a pattern of gesturing is deemed appropriate by a specific culture.

For instance, Europeans use gestures relatively frequently to enhance what they are saying, often described as if they are talking with their hands. Asians, on the other hand, do not use many gestures. In the United States, gesturing when accompanying speech adds emphasis to specific phrases and makes the speaker appear more animated. If I were to describe a place that I had been to recently, a mountainside with a vertical drop that was significant, I would probably use a gesture to show you the vertical drop. I would use a flat hand and extended arm and move it downward to show you how severe the drop was. People in the United States frequently use hand motions to 'show' you what they are describing.

Gestures can also be used to express emotions—anger, excitement, sadness, for example. If a person has just seen a car accident, the person may express verbally how they saw the accident while either covering their mouth with a flat hand or holding a flat hand over their chest. These gestures express shock. Another example would be if a person was frustrated and could not figure something out after trying a particular task for a while. The person may hold their head with both hands or make a fist and move it downwards quickly. You may or may not use these gestures to express how you feel, but you should understand them when you see others making them while here in the United States. Learning what particular gestures mean will help you better understand people in the United States as they give you clues as to how they are feeling. You would be better off staying away from someone who has just expressed they are frustrated, as they may not be in the best mood to approach…unless of course you want to offer assistance.

Cathryn Cushner Edelstein

Gesturing without speech:

If someone is talking with you and gesturing, it isn't difficult to understand what their gestures mean. However, if they are gesturing while silent, it is important to take the time to understand their movements. Their body is giving you clues about their mood, the way they are feeling, and if they are open to talking or not. A tense person will have rigid body movements, while a relaxed person will not. Clues like this give you a signal as to whether you should approach a person or not.

As a teacher, when I see a student sitting quietly with their head in their hands, looking down, and shaking their head left to right, I know that this means they don't understand something, are overwhelmed, or frustrated and upset. I would probably approach this student and immediately ask if everything was all right. Likewise, a student slouched in her chair tapping her pen on her desk quickly shows that she may be nervous. She may be unprepared for class and feels anxious. Watching these gestures definitely helps to understand how someone is feeling.

It is impossible to list all the gestures we use in the United States, but I have selected a few that are commonly confusing to foreign students I work with:

1. Fist closed and thumb up: Great! Wonderful!
2. Fist closed and thumb down: Not good. Negative.
3. Fist closed, and knocking on your head lightly twice or knocking on actual wood: superstitious thing to do—people in the United States say "knock on wood" or actually do it, if they want a wish to come true.
4. Holding the thumb tip and pointer finger together to form an 'O' means 'okay' or 'good.'
5. Rubbing the thumb together with all four finger tips with the hand faced upwards 'money.' If someone does this to you, they are asking for money or telling you that something costs a lot of money.
6. If someone wants you to come closer, they will either wave backwards towards themselves or use their pointer finger waving towards them. If they want you to go away, they will wave towards you throwing their finger tips downwards.
7. If someone moves their pointer finger in front of their neck like they are drawing a line across it, they are indicating they have

had enough of something, to stop.

8. If they point their pointer finger in the air and move it around circularly pointing upwards next to their head, they are using this to sarcastically indicate they are excited—meaning they really aren't exited.

9. Holding up the middle finger is an obscene gesture that means 'go to hell.' This is referred to as 'flipping the bird' or 'giving someone the finger.'

10. Using the pointer and middle finger on both hands to simulate the symbol for "quotations." This gesture is used when either quoting something said by another person, or used in a sarcastic manner when saying something cynically. It should only be used casually in conversation and never in formal settings.

▪ **Manners**

While I am on the topic of gestures, I think it is a good time to explain which gestures are considered good manners in the United States. Manners, or correct behavior in certain situations, are necessary if you are to represent yourself as a considerate, polished, and caring person. Manners, like everything I have discussed, are different throughout the world. I have been in situations with clients that have made me feel uncomfortable because their concept of proper behavior is different than mine. One afternoon I arrived at a company in Boston to meet with a client. We sat together facing each other and within minutes he burped loudly, directly towards me. He didn't apologize or say, "Excuse me." He thought it was perfectly all right to do this. I did not. In America, this is considered very rude. I am aware that in other cultures, this is fine, but in the United States it is not. One should always cover their mouth and turn their head away from another person when burping. Ideally, one should not burp altogether near another person but sometimes this cannot be avoided.

Here is a list of common manners or accepted behaviors in the United States:

1. When greeting someone, it is wise to offer a strong handshake. This is advisable between both genders. Kissing a stranger is never accepted unless it is between relatives.

2. Yawning, burping or coughing requires the person, who is

Cathryn Cushner Edelstein

doing so, to cover their mouth and turn away from other people. Flatulence in public is not polite.

3. When sitting down for a meal, it is proper behavior to take the napkin and put it on one's lap before and during a meal. It is also expected that one will use the silverware/utensils offered to eat the meal. Using one's hands to eat items that are supposed to be eaten with utensils is not appropriate.

4. Unless arrangements have been made prior to a meal being eaten at a restaurant, it is expected that the people at the meal will offer to pay their portion of the meal. (It is perfectly fine to leave food on one's plate; unnecessary to eat everything.)

5. Chew with your mouth closed.

6. Cleaning one's teeth in front of others is considered rude.

7. Crossing one's legs is fine, but if a female is wearing a skirt, she should make sure that her skirt is pulled down over her upper thighs.

8. Grooming (brushing hair, clipping nails etc.) around food is never a good thing.

9. Cell phone usage (texting and talking) in classrooms, theaters, libraries, restaurants, and during conversations with others is deemed impolite. Best to turn phones off or place them in the silent mode. When you need to use your cell phone, you should walk out of the arena to use it.

10. If one is entering or leaving through a doorway, it is customary to hold the door open for the next person passing through.

11. Using the phrases "Please," "Thank you," and "No, thank you" are appreciated and show good manners. I cannot emphasize this enough!

12. Waiting in lines or cues is what Americans do. Always go to the end of a line; never try to 'cut' a line by forcing your way in. Americans get very angry and you will most likely be verbally scolded for doing so.

13. Personal hygiene is very important in the United States. People bathe daily and use deodorant regularly. In addition, most women shave their legs and underarms, as hairiness is viewed more of a male tendency.

CHAPTER 3

COMMUNICATION FOR SPECIFIC SITUATIONS

Language is easily separated into two categories: receptive language (reading and listening), and productive language (writing and speaking). Reading and listening can be learned and improved by using textbooks and audio/video segments, but productive language is best taught and practiced using realistic speaking and writing situations. Many of my foreign students feel fairly comfortable with their English receptive language skills, but uncomfortable with their productive language skills and their knowledge of what is expected in particular social situations. In this chapter, I will place an emphasis on productive language skills while explaining what expectations are in place in particular institutional and social situations. To make this easier, they will be organized by use.

■ School/Classroom Communication

Depending on where you come from, the behavior deemed acceptable in the school you attended was either interactive or passive.

Interactive: Students and teachers interact with each other in classes. Commonly teachers will ask a question and students raise their hands to answer. Individual and group presentations are common and students work in groups on assignments/projects in and out of the classroom.

Passive: Students are expected to sit quietly in their seats and listen to the teacher. Students are not required to answer questions, permitted to ask questions, or make presentations. Assignments are completed individually, usually without an oral component.

In the United States, classes are typically interactive. There are situations where classes are taught lecture style, which is more passive, but overall teachers and students converse throughout classes, with rules for behavior understood by all. These rules include: 1) students raising their hands and waiting to be called on by a teacher to speak, 2) students raising their hands when they have a question or need clarification, and 3) students working in groups with others in the classroom cooperatively and inclusively.

Depending on the teacher and the constraints of a classroom, seating in a typical classroom can be either in rows, circles, semi-circles, or around tables. Teachers with moveable chairs can arrange the classroom how they want, often taking into consideration how communication will take place in that class. A class that is set up in rows is considered more formal and is fairly standard, but it is not uncommon to find the chairs arranged in the other formations to foster more interactive communication. It is important to note that no matter how the chairs are arranged, teachers usually will still require a student to raise their hand in order to speak.

How to respond to a question or ask a question in class

It is very common for teachers to ask students questions in order to make sure students understand material that was either given as homework or newly learned. From an early age, beginning in kindergarten at age five, students have learned to share their knowledge with the class and the teachers by doing this. Students will eagerly raise their hands to be called on—sometimes very enthusiastically. In most cases, the teacher is not concerned about whether the answer is correct or not, but most likely wants the students to 'try' and will move on to another student to answer if the previous attempt was incorrect. Many times, a student who doesn't raise their hand will be called on. This is done to try to emphasize inclusion and to attend to students who may be shy or less confident.

Likewise, if you have a question or need some clarification, don't hesitate to raise your hand! We have an expression in the United States, "The only stupid question is the one that you didn't ask," so instead of becoming frustrated, ask a question. If you find that you have a lot of questions, or are experiencing complete confusion, make an appointment to meet with your teacher.

Cathryn Cushner Edelstein

Private meetings with teachers are common and acceptable. In fact, it is a great way for you to get to know your teacher more personally and vice versa.

You may not have experience in an interactive classroom, and it may take some time for you to feel confident enough to participate actively. I suggest you try. So many times students have told me they feel scared and afraid they won't say the right thing, or that their English will not be understood by fellow students and teachers. Don't worry so much about this. Just do it. The more practice you have, the easier it will become. To be successful in an American classroom, you need to jump in and become involved. This is part of the American learning experience and to do it successfully you will need to interact.

▪ Restaurants – Food and Protocol

As the United States is known as a melting pot – it has restaurants that reflect the diversity of the people who live here. In major cities and in suburbs alike, one can find food that encompasses many ethnicities. Whether Chinese, Middle Eastern, Spanish, Turkish, Japanese or any other, a quick search will result in finding a place that serves almost any type of food. Many are authentic, that is, they are owned by people of a particular ethnicity/culture, but ethnic food can be served in typical American restaurants as well. Menus in the United States are diverse and chefs prepare food that spans the globe. There is no such thing as 'American only' food because of the diversity of people who live here, so even though a restaurant may look to be nonethnic, it may in fact serve some ethnic dishes. It is important to note that if you are planning a visit to a rural American town, choices may be more limited as people who live there are more homogeneous. The menu will most likely reflect grilled or fried food and pasta dishes.

Many restaurants in the United States require reservations, but typically one can walk in and expect to be seated with little or no waiting time. When calling ahead to make reservations, you will need to know when you want to be seated and how many people are in your group. In addition, the restaurant will need your name to reserve a table. Make sure to spell your name clearly so the person can understand it. *Remembering to use a varied intonation pattern will help you—begin with the first letter at the highest pitch and each letter following that one should gradually be lower in pitch than the last.* This same technique should be used when ordering 'take-out' (ordering food to pick up or be delivered), which will aid in clear communication between you and the person taking your order. Many of my students have shared that communicating via telephone in English is very difficult. This is because there are no nonverbal cues accompanying the conversation. Using varied intonation will help and always remember to ask the person on the other end to repeat back to you what they think you ordered. This will guarantee you get what you asked for. There is nothing worse than getting your order and discovering it isn't what you wanted. If you want to avoid communicating via telephone, some restaurants have online ordering, and you can use your computer to order, but most do not.

Tipping, or giving the server a monetary reward for good service, is customary in most restaurants and bars in the United States. Do not tip at fast food restaurants, but do at most others. The amount of a tip is determined by the cost of the total food ordered before state tax is applied. State tax is different for every state and ranges from 1% to 10% depending on which state you are in when you make your purchase.

Tipping guidelines: for excellent service, tip the waiter 18% to 20%; for good service, 15%; and for less favorable service, 10% to 15%. Waiters in the United States make very little money per hour, less than the legal hourly wage, because it is expected they will earn most of their money in tips. Please be aware of this and reward the service you received appropriately.

Common Types of Restaurants in the United States

The atmosphere, service style, and price of a meal at a restaurant often depend on the style of the restaurant you go to. The five most common types of restaurants are described below:

Fast food restaurants are just as they sound: fast, inexpensive, and more about eating quickly than the eating experience. McDonalds, Burger King, and Kentucky Fried Chicken are just a few. You may have seen these around your native country, and many students have told me the U.S. menus at these places are very different from those seen in their native countries. Typical food items are hamburgers and fried food such as chicken and French fries. Drive-thru ordering is common at fast food restaurants but you can also order from the counter and eat inside.

Pizza (Peet-tsah) restaurants are all over the United States. Most people call ahead and order pizza for take-out dining. Occasionally, there is seating to eat the pizza inside the restaurant. Pizza, because it can be custom ordered with many types of toppings, its cost, and its value, is one of the most commonly eaten foods in the United States. Pizza is traditionally cooked in large ovens at most take-out pizza places, but brick ovens or stone hearths are used as well in more formal eateries that serve pizza.

Casual or family-style restaurants are priced more moderately, have extensive menus, and are often part of 'chains,' meaning the same named restaurant has many locations. Of course, there are many casual restaurants that are owned and operated by individuals as well. Often the name of a restaurant will give you a hint as to what they serve. Modifications to food that appears on a menu can usually be made within limits. Don't be afraid ask your waiter if you want to change something about the way a meal is prepared. For example, if a dish is described as being sautéed in butter and you would rather not have it prepared this way, ask the waiter what other choices you have. Also, if the menu states a dish comes with French fries and you would rather have a vegetable instead, just ask. These are accommodations that are often made, and the chefs are prepared for these requests. You are the customer after all, and the restaurant will want to please you.

A **café** usually requires that diners order their food from a person at a counter and then sit down to eat. Prices vary and are usually inexpensive. Sandwiches, bakery items, coffee, and tea are typically served in a café. The menus at cafés are limited and accommodations as to how they are prepared can often be made. There are chains of cafés throughout the United States, but you may find some that are individually owned. Many have Internet access, and one can sit and casually dine and/or sip a drink for a long while.

A **fine-dining restaurant** will serve a more gourmet menu. Items on the menu can be expensive, but the preparation and 'plating' (the way the food is placed on a plate) will be more stylish and complex. Sauces, spices, and methods of preparation make the food more extravagant and unique. Menus at these restaurants will change seasonally to allow for the freshest ingredients. Shortly after being seated, a waiter may come to your table to announce special meals the chef is preparing that day that do not appear on your menu. If the waiter doesn't mention the cost of these, don't be shy about asking for it. The waiters at finer restaurants are very attentive to diners' needs, and accommodations to how food is prepared are readily made. You may desire that something be prepared without butter or without a particular sauce. The waiter is familiar with these requests and will usually oblige. Reservations are most always required and must be made in advance of a week.

It is important to note:

The minimum age to drink alcohol in the United States is 21. Do not be surprised if you are asked to show identification of your age when ordering an alcoholic beverage. This is done to protect the establishment, as they are liable for serving alcohol to minors. Their license to serve alcohol is contingent on obeying this law. In addition, a bartender may cease to serve someone they feel has had too much to drink. They are liable for serving someone too much alcohol as well. If you are from a country where you were able to drink alcohol and you no longer can, this will be a big change for you. You should be warned that buying or consuming alcohol younger than the age of 21 is a criminal offense in the United States.

Smoking in restaurants is prohibited in most towns across the United States. Each town is able to establish its own laws regarding smoking.

▪ Social Gatherings

The Invitation   What does RSVP mean?

Invitations to parties, dinners, engagement parties (premarital), weddings, and most other types of social gatherings may come in the mail, emailed, or via telephone. The invitation will specify the date, time, and place. Also commonly included is the acronym,

RSVP - French for, répondez s'il vous plait–that indicates who you should contact to confirm you can either attend or not and the deadline to respond by. For example, if the RSVP states: Samantha Smith 888-555-1111 June 29, 2012, this means you should contact Samantha before June 29, 2012. This information helps the host plan for their party. We also use the phrase RSVP as another way of saying 'responded to an invitation.' So, if some asks you if you have RSVP'd yet, they are asking if you have responded yet. Replying to an invitation is courteous and expected. Not doing so is considered rude, and the host may contact you to find out why you didn't respond. If you have responded that you can attend and find that you need to cancel for any reason, you should let your host know right away. Not showing up when you responded that you would be there is not considered good manners, so let your host know.

BYOB? Pot Luck? Hors d'oeuvre?

Also on the invitation, you may see BYOB, an acronym that means 'bring your own bottle' (beer or liquor); pot luck, which means bring some food for everyone to share; or bring an hors d'oeuvre, an appetizer or starter for sharing.

If you receive an invitation asking you to bring something, you need to make a decision as to what you'll bring…

BYOB – bring a six-pack of beer, a bottle of wine, or a bottle of liquor. If you bring something that you would like to drink, you can usually open it and consume it at the party. Expect that what you bring will either be shared by all those attending the party or kept by the host if it is not consumed.

Pot luck – bring an appetizer, a salad, a main course dish, a side dish, or a dessert to share with all the guests at the gathering. You can bring it on a disposable plate or a glass plate that you take back home with you after the party. It is nice to bring serving utensils as well in case the host does not have the proper utensils to use when serving. You may ask the host ahead of time what part of the meal they would like you to bring, as they often know what other guests will be bringing and want to make sure the same dishes are not being brought by multiple guests.

Hors d'oeuvres – bring a dip with chips or vegetables, a block of cheese with crackers, or anything that is small enough to be eaten with either a toothpick or one's fingers. Make sure what you bring is ready to eat and on a serving plate that can be used.

When to arrive?

The type of gathering, and what was printed on the invitation determines the expected arrival time of guests. If you are attending a wedding or other ceremony, you should arrive at least fifteen minutes early to make sure you are seated before it begins. Ceremonies in the United States begin on time, and there is nothing more awkward than arriving during or after the main event has happened.

If you are attending a private party, a dinner party, or a casual party, the time of day indicated on the invitation is not a suggestion, but a real time when the party will begin. In keeping with the term, 'arriving fashionably late,' arriving around 15 minutes late is acceptable, arriving much later than that is not appropriate.

If the invitation stated it is 'an open house' gathering, the time it will begin and end are printed on the invitation. You can arrive at any time within the times given, though arriving at the end is not advisable. Usually people tend to arrive during the earlier part of the gathering. If food is offered, the selection may be greatly depleted near the end of the party.

What to wear?

The occasion and venue will determine what you should wear, and often the invitation will also indicate wardrobe requirements/dress code.

Casual – Wear anything you think will be appropriate.

Dressy casual – Jeans, shorts and sneakers are not appropriate. Men are expected to wear dress pants with collared shirt, with or without a jacket, and women should wear dress pants or a skirt/dress.

Cocktail – Women in evening dresses or dress pants and blouses, and men in dark suits.

Black tie optional – Men should wear dark suits with ties or tuxedos, and women should wear gowns or cocktail attire.

Black tie – Men wear tuxedos, and women wear gowns or cocktail attire.

Cathryn Cushner Edelstein

Gifts

When invited to someone's house for a party, it is customary to bring a gift for the host. A bouquet of flowers, a bottle of wine, or small house gift is common. If you are invited to a formal party in honor of someone's birthday or to an engagement party or wedding, a more generous gift is necessary. Birthday gifts are often very personal and should reflect what you know the person enjoys. Engagement and wedding gifts are usually purchased for the couple's future home needs, and often couples register with certain stores to help guests choose a gift. Gift registries are often used in the United States for weddings and baby showers so the recipients can indicate their needs and be assured they are getting what they want. You can ask a couple where they are registered to get this information if you would like to use a registry.

▪ Grocery Shopping

There are several types of grocery stores in the United States, and the availability of them differs depending on where you live. Convenience markets, specialty food shops, farm stands, and large grocery stores/supermarkets are available in most suburbs and cities. However, more rural places have more limited choices. There has been a shift towards eating healthier, organic food in recent years, so with this movement, health food supermarkets have also cropped up. Americans have become obsessed with fat content and healthy eating, though Americans are still some of the most overweight people around. All packaged food has labels that list fat content and calories. The government requires this information be made public for consumers. From dairy products to meats, you will notice this. At first it may seem confusing to decipher, but once you get used to it, you will learn what the labels mean and how the taste of food can change depending on fat content. The terms 'nonfat,' 'low fat,' and 'whole fat,' appear on many products and alter taste, as well as the calories.

Convenience markets – These are found in suburbs, cities, and rural areas alike. They usually do not carry fresh food, but rather canned, frozen, and boxed food. They are usually open early and close late at night. Some even stay open twenty-four hours a day. Typically the prices at these markets are higher than in larger stores, but their convenient hours of operation and location do make them handy.

Farm stands/farmers markets – Throughout the United States, fresh food is grown and shipped to stores all over. In some areas, the farms open a shop on their premises and sell their fresh goods directly to consumers. The experience of shopping at a farm is like nothing else, you can smell and touch many assortments of greens, fruit, grains, and herbs. If you can't grow your own, this is the next best thing. In many cities and suburbs, farmers markets are organized once per week during summer months. Farms from near and far rent booths and tables to sell their specialties. If you can't get to a farm, this is the next best thing. Often, the same farms come back week after week so you can count on what will be available. Make sure to look for postings in your area to find the schedule of when a farmers market is coming to a location near you.

Grocery stores/supermarkets – Most people in the United States use these terms interchangeably because they offer just about anything you may want to eat or cook. Supermarkets are typically arranged the same way. A traditional grocery store has a fish market, a meat/fowl section, a deli section, a fresh produce section, a bakery, and a dairy section. The store has aisles throughout that sell items in bags, boxes and jars. Fresh and frozen food is found around the perimeter of supermarkets, while boxed, bagged, and canned food is found in the aisles. Also found in the aisles are paper goods and assorted hygiene products such as shampoo, medical necessities, and greeting cards. Some supermarkets also sell prepared food that simply requires heating or can be eaten as-is.

Tips for making the most of your shopping experience:

Sales and Discounts

Most grocery stores offer customer shopping cards that allow the customer to take advantage of sales and discounts. Without these cards, the discount is not taken off the price of the goods being purchased. It is wise to obtain a shopping card for each store you plan to visit. If you don't have a card, ask the cashier if

Cathryn Cushner Edelstein

you can apply for one. They often oblige and you get your goods at a lower price. People also obtain discounts by bringing in paper coupons that are found in local newspapers. In order to use a coupon, make sure the requirement for use is met—some may ask you to buy two of the same item to get the discount while others may require the product be of a certain weight or size.

At the Deli Counter

Sliced meats and cheeses are found in the deli section. The people who work behind the counter will take your order and slice the brand, type, and quantity of the product you desire. The assortment can be overwhelming, especially if you have never purchased food this way. First, know that people are waited on in the order they arrived at the counter. Often, a number machine will be there. Take a number if there is one, or you will never have your turn to order. Numbers are flashed on a monitor on the wall of the deli so you can see which number is being served at any given time. If a number machine is not available, look around and take note of who was there when you arrived and who came after. The deli person will simply call out, "Who's next?" and if it's your turn, you should hold your hand up and say, "I am."

When it's your turn, you should already have in mind what it is you want. You can ask for a sample of any product you think you may want to order; ask for one slice of something to try it and see if you like it. For example, if you want some roasted turkey breast but there are several brands, ask for a sample of a couple of them. You can eat a sample right there and make a decision based on your liking. Order deli meat and cheese by requesting portions of a pound – 1/3, 1/2, 3/4, or a full pound. Since the meat is not packaged with preservatives, the meat usually doesn't last for more than a few days, so plan accordingly.

At the Seafood Counter

Fish and other seafood (shell fish) are shipped to supermarkets locally and globally. It isn't unusual to find tuna that has been flown in from Asia or salmon from the west coast. Of course these are shipped frozen and are flash frozen; which means they were frozen soon after the catch, right on the boat. Unlike other countries, fish is not sold alive, except for lobster. The cost of fish ranges from moderate to expensive in supermarkets and is plentiful. Ordering is much like at the deli counter, you may have to take a number or pay attention as to when you arrived so you can keep track of when it will be your turn to order. In addition, you can either order a whole piece of fish as it appears in the case or you can ask the person behind the counter to cut a specific size for you. Once again, as at the deli counter, you order fish by portions of a pound. If you are unsure how much to order, let the person behind the counter know how many will be dining, and they can usually assist you in determining how much you will need. A conversation between you and the fish clerk is necessary for you to make the purchase.

At the Bakery

Unlike a specialty bakery, which only sells what is made fresh each day, the supermarket bakery sells items they make on the premises, as well as items shipped to them from commercial bakeries. Breads, muffins, cakes, and cookies are all for sale. For a special occasion, a birthday cake can be personalized at no cost. If you are in need of a birthday cake, this is the most cost-effective place to find one—just choose a cake and ask the person at the counter to write the name of the person to be honored on the cake in frosting. For more elaborate custom cake orders, you will need to give them a few days notice, but you can walk in and buy a simple personalized cake within a moment's notice.

The Meat/Fowl Section

Butchers are commonly on hand at supermarkets. Although the array of products available is plentiful, if you have a question or would like a special cut of meat, you can ask the butcher to assist you. While choosing chicken, meat, or turkey, look for the 'sell by' date; this is a date printed on each package that indicates freshness expiration. Beyond that date, the food will no longer be edible, so be careful with your choices. If something is set to expire soon, you can freeze it to make it last longer. It is not recommended that meat and fowl be frozen for more than six months.

Something that often confuses my students is the label on the packaging that explains fat content. For example, a number of 80/20 on a package of hamburger meat means its fat-to-lean ratio

Cathryn Cushner Edelstein

is 80% lean and 20% fat. The higher the first number, the less fat it contains. An additional label may indicate the meat or fowl is organic, free range, or steroid free. An explanation of these terms can be found below in the paragraph on health food stores. (Supermarkets occasionally offer these healthier options for meat and fowl.)

Dairy

The refrigerated dairy area is loaded with milk, cheese, yogurt, and butter. This may seem simple enough, but when you add in the multiple variations of fat content into the mix, the options can be overwhelming. On a recent visit to a supermarket with a few students, they asked me what type of milk they should buy. I answered by asking them how watery or creamy they like their milk. Nonfat milk is very watery; 2% milk, also called low-fat milk, a little less so; and whole milk is creamier. If you are lactose intolerant, which means you cannot drink milk because of allergies, there is soymilk and lactose-free milk. Of course, there is cream, too, which is very heavy and thick compared to whole milk, and there are variations of that, too. The choices are endless when it not only comes to milk, but to yogurt, cheese, ice cream, and cheese, too. The same fat content options apply to nearly all dairy products so look closely to make sure you are buying what you want. Also, note that some products are not what they seem. For example, there are sticks of what may look like butter on the butter shelf, but they are really vegetable oil shaped like butter. Read carefully and remember, the only way you will really learn what you like is to try different options.

Fresh Produce

Fruit and vegetables are available to purchase either prepackaged or by the pound. You can buy by the piece or buy many pieces when you buy by the pound. Look for scales hanging near the produce to weigh what you have chosen so you will know how much it costs. The price is by the pound and should be clearly marked near each bin the produce came from. Wash the produce before you eat it, as it has passed through many hands before yours.

Shopping at a large supermarket is an experience. You will be amazed at the items you can find there and how many choices exist. Americans take pride in being able to make choices, and no place is this more obvious than at a supermarket. Now that you have some basic information to help guide you, it should not be such an overwhelming experience. The people who work at these markets are used to people asking a lot of questions, so if you have any, don't be afraid to ask.

Health Food Supermarkets

Throughout the United States, supermarkets that sell only natural and/or organic food have presented shoppers with yet another choice of places to buy food. These stores are generally more expensive but some think well worth the extra cost. At these markets, you can find meats, dairy, seafood, fruit, and produce that have been certified by the USDA (United States Department of Agriculture) as either natural or organic. Many use these labels interchangeably, but they don't mean the same thing. According to the USDA, 'natural' means it is minimally processed and free of synthetic hormones, antibiotics, and hydrogenated oils. 'Organic' mainly has to do with the way the food was produced. Organic farmers must adhere to specific requirements: livestock must have access to the outdoors and not be given growth hormones or antibiotics, they must use recycling methods, and they must not use synthetic pesticides. In addition, organic farms recycle and promote biodiversity. Crops are not grown with synthetic pesticides, bioengineered genes, or petroleum-based fertilizers. [1] The other description often used in these markets is 'free-range,' which means the livestock was not caged on the farm and had freedom to move around. For example, free-range eggs means the chickens who laid the eggs were not caged.

In addition, health food supermarkets also cater to people with food allergies. They often have many foods that do not contain specific allergens. For example, if one has a gluten (wheat) allergy, this type of food store will carry many items that are labeled gluten-free.

If you have food allergies, a health food store may be what you desire. However, check the regular supermarket first because they have some health food there, and the prices are far less expensive. As far as the store layout, the design of these stores is similar to

Cathryn Cushner Edelstein

the regular supermarket, with all of the same counters and areas where food is sold. You will still have to speak with the store clerks at the counters to get service, and the general process for selecting and purchasing food is the same.

CHAPTER 4

In Their Own Words

In this chapter you can read responses to a survey I posted online and in my classes. They are real comments from students who are now in the United States studying. You may find students from your area of the world or from a culture similar to your own. Hopefully, their comments will help you prepare for your experience in the United States.

International students studying in the United States were asked:

1) From a communication perspective, what did you think it would be like to study in the United States BEFORE you came? (Language – speaking & comprehension, comfort with the classroom teaching style, making friends, etc.)

2) From a communication perspective, how did your prior thoughts differ from the experience you had while studying in the United States?

1. Francine   *From: Puerto Rico   Native Language: Spanish*

"I thought that my vast experience with the American education system and culture would give me an edge. I thought that making friends would be a lot easier for me because I have pretty good communication skills."

"It has been a lot harder than what I thought to communicate with people from different cultures. You have to be mindful of what you say—make sure they understand the context and remember to always be respectful of their cultures. It was very hard to make friends. It did not happen as quickly as I thought or wanted to. It took a while to get to know each other to really create a friend bond."

2. Bellah   *From: Zambia   Native Language: Nyanja*

"I thought I knew English well enough to be able to communicate with people of different nationalities. I had prior experience studying in Europe so I thought I would easily adapt."

"Most times I had to repeat myself a couple times and even change my pronunciation before I could be understood. This made me too self-conscious."

3. Yi   *From: China   Native Language: Chinese*

"I thought campus life would be crazy and that people would have trouble understanding my English. I thought I would be isolated because I am Asian. I also imagined that school would be horrible because I am not used to the free discussion teaching style and I would be uncomfortable speaking English in front of the whole class."

"My first culture shock was the way Americans greet each other. They ask how you are but then walk away. I took this personally, that they didn't want to be friends with me. I later realized that this is just part of their culture. American students are generally very friendly and polite."

4. Luis   *From: Philippines   Native Language: Filipino*

"When I decided to attend graduate school in the United States, I expected a shift in the teaching style. Coming from very strict classrooms, I was excited for 'open-style' teaching methods. I wasn't at all scared about talking in classes since classes were taught in English where I come from."

"Not disappointed. I found that the 'open-style' of teaching and discussions were very conducive to learning. All thoughts and opinions are heard and discussed."

Cathryn Cushner Edelstein

5. Torpad   *From: Thailand   Native Language: Thai*

"I thought it would be challenging because English is not my first language. I knew I would be able to communicate in everyday life, but not so sure about communicating formally in the classroom. I wondered if I would have to use technical terms for presentations, if I would fit in, and would I know how to talk and be friends with Americans."

"When I actually got to America, I found it very easy to talk with Americans because they are nice. They are friendlier than I thought they would be. Classes are not as difficult as I thought they would be. I was scared to speak up in class because I never had to speak a word in class back home. Here in the U.S., I must be brave and speak my thoughts out loud. It gets better over time. I just need to be confident and believe that my ideas are worth something and remind myself that it is okay to be wrong."

6. Radka   *From: Czech Republic   Native Language: Czech*

"When I first went to study in the United States, I went to a small town in Tennessee as an exchange student. I thought I would make a lot of friends and everyone would be eager to learn about a different culture. However, that did not really happen. What I found out later was that people from my classes did not have the courage to start a conversation although they really wanted to talk to me."

"Making new friends was easier when I later moved, to go to school in a city. I took a class offered to international students where I made a lot of friends. Don't be afraid to start talking to people from your classes. Do not feel discouraged if you feel like any of your first conversations do not help you find your next best friend."

7. Prudence   *From: Swaziland   Native Language: Siswati*

"I thought it might be easier for me because we use British English from kindergarten in my country."

"I was made to believe that the USA was just 'Perfect', a melting pot and culture sensitive. But I was surprised by a lot of things, like the differences between education in different states and the quality of education between private and public schools."

8. Vipavee   *From: Thailand   Native Language: Thai*

"First of all I heard from other people that studying in the U.S. required a lot of class participation. You have to speak up and share your ideas. However, I thought class attendance was not that important. I was also worried about group work. I thought that it would be hard to communicate with Americans. I was afraid my thoughts would not be respected."

"Class participation is extremely important here because they want you to share different ideas, especially if you are from a different part of the world. There is no problem doing group work with Americans, especially when you work with very nice people. Some Americans love to learn about different cultures, and they appreciate it if you share your culture with them."

9. Kento   *From: Japan   Native Language: Japanese*

"I was excited to study in the United States as it is the political and economic center of the world. I hoped to meet different people from different parts of the world."

"When I moved to the United States, I did meet people from around the world, but the people were not so different from me."

10. Divya   *From: India   Native Language: Hindi*

"I thought it would be hard making friends as most students would be American. I also felt that it would be hard communicating with other students, understanding their humor etc. I also thought writing in English would be challenging."

"College has been pretty easy for me. I am having problems writing essays, but apart from that the teachers are pretty cooperative and helpful. Making friends is easy as American students are more open than kids back home. I'm having a great time."

11. Alexia   *From: Greece   Native Language: Greek*

"I thought that professors wouldn't really care about each student personally and wouldn't care if students attended class or were struggling."

"Students can talk with their professors privately during office hours, and they really do care about their students. This creates a better work environment for both students and professors."

12. Ran   *From: China   Native Language: Chinese*

"I thought the biggest difficulty I would meet would be the language problem. For my oral English is not so good. I was afraid it may generate some negative influences on making new friends in U.S."

"I think the language problem does bring some difficulties but not as serious as I imagined. But I think there are less channels to make friends with native students."

13. Melodi *From: Turkey Native Language: Turkish*

"Like most people coming from a third world country, I always thought of the U.S. as a country where dreams come true. Applying to college in the U.S. was therefore in a way, a pursuit of my dreams. I had mixed feelings though. I didn't know if I would be able to adapt or make friends easily. I really doubted myself. On the other hand, I was really excited to start a new life in a new place, studying what I love."

"My college experience so far has been great. All of my doubts have faded as I have made a lot of good friends and have adapted to my environment. People have been friendly. If I get lost on a street, someone always stops to ask me what is wrong and tries to help me. That is what I like the most here. It has been a great experience."

14. Laura *From: Mexico Native Language: Spanish*

"I wanted to come to the United States because I know the U.S. has a great education system. I always thought it would be hard to deal with the language barriers."

"The language barrier wasn't so hard to overcome. The thing that can be disconcerting is how culturally specific education programs can be. All you need is a little bit of patience and to ask questions when you need to. Although a lot of knowledge is assumed, asking for help brings out the best in people, and faculty and students will help you in any way they can."

15. Mahesh *From: India Native Language: Hindi*

"Coming from an American school in India, I did not expect a great deal of difference. I felt that the courses I had taken in high school would be similar to the courses I would be taking in the United States in terms of style and structure."

"Everything from popular culture to pronunciation is expected at a different level given that my American high school was located in Asia. The level of expectation is much higher in the United States. Pronunciation issues are not as acceptable here."

16. Jing   *From: China   Native Language: Chinese*

"Before going to the United States, I thought my English was not so bad and there would be no problem. I also thought classes wouldn't be that hard, maybe only reading books. I expected interactive classrooms and that classmates would be friendly to people from other countries."

"After I got to the United States, I found the oral English I learned in China was only the basics. It is hard to communicate very deeply with people. A lot of things that I use in daily life, I can't name, and that is embarrassing. Some people are friendly, mostly older people. Seems people don't have much interest in learning things from other countries."

17. AbdulRafiu   *From: Nigeria   Native Language: Hausa*

"I thought studying in the United States would be like a journey to 'paradise on earth' where everything works out well. I later discovered that making friends and keeping track of how the educational system operates is a challenge."

"My thoughts and what I experienced differed completely. The greatest challenge was homesickness and to this day, I still find it hard to comprehend why people will have little to do with each other compared to the communal system where I grew up."

18. Chau   *From: Vietnam   Native Language: Vietnamese*

"I was concerned with language communication, culture learning, ways of learning."

"I have learned a lot from studying here. The ways of teaching and learning have helped me become more active in class participation, and to be more professionally and scientifically organized in working and thinking."

19. Nazaire   *From: The Republic of Congo*
Native Language: French

"I thought communication and education would be different than what it is like in my country. And that it would take me a little while to get adjusted to the change. I also thought that I'd have language problems."

"I had little language issues at the beginning. The longer I stay, the easier I understand people in different situations."

20. Saerom   *From: South Korea   Native Language: Korean*

"It would be intense due to the language barrier. I knew there would be a huge cultural gap too, and I was worried about it, especially with classroom culture. I heard the difference between Asian and American classroom culture is that American classes are more discussion-focused while Asian ones are lecture-focused. What I worried most about was not following professors' lectures and about getting into fast-paced discussions because I thought my English-speaking was poorer than listening."

"It was hard at the beginning, I was terrified after the first class. It seemed no one understood what I was talking about and I gave up. I later learned that even with just simple changing of intonation, I could communicate with people much easier. Also, there were lots of differences in pronunciation and speaking manner from what I learned in my country. I still have many friends from Asia who do not believe 'h' of 'herb' is a mute letter. So with two years of studying in the USA I see myself improving really fast. The most important part I think is, I have a confidence now. So I'm trying to speak and make people understand what I'm talking about without fear even though my English is still not perfect."

21. Huiju   *From: Taiwan   Native Language: Chinese*

"Before coming to America, I was worried about communication problems. I was afraid that people would speak English so quickly that I wouldn't be able to understand. I was worried that I wouldn't be able to express my thoughts in class because it took me some time to process the language. I thought people would be impatient when I spoke slowly."

"In the beginning, I actually had a problem understanding English spoken quickly. Sometimes I felt embarrassed to ask people to repeat what they said. Then the strategy I used was to say what I understood to make sure I was on the right track. After a period of time, I became used to the speed of their speaking. I know I have to practice speaking English as much as I can. Therefore, I speak English with my Taiwanese roommates in my apartment. The more I speak, the more fluent English I speak."

22. Ketan   *From: India   Native Language: Hindi*

"I knew coming in that it could be challenging getting into a global environment with people from all over the world. Though, from a communication perspective, I did not expect much friction."

"Over the last two academic years, I've spent more time communicating with people from all across the globe and making them understand my thoughts and understanding theirs. Patience is the key. Altering pronunciation, knowing slang and idioms, and just good listening skills can be really helpful."

23. Hattan   *From: Saudi Arabia   Native Language: Arabic*

"I thought that there would be a good chance to meet with students from different nationalities, learn about new cultures and listen to different points of view..."

"I found that studying was almost as I anticipated. I liked that most of the classes were discussion based and interactive..."

24. Allen   *From: Taiwan   Native Language: Chinese*

"Interact with others and learn from different perspectives."

"Language proficiency is the key to achievement, even more than what I thought before."

25. Boda   *From: China   Native Language: Chinese*

"Before, I regarded American people as open-minded, extroverts, and kind people. They would be ambitious and willing to explore. From a communication point of view, the discussions that I was going to be [having] with American students would have some obstacles since culture shocks exist."

"In fact, some of the American students are very patient while they are trying to explain topics. They have no knowledge about the topics they are not interested in, which is very different compared with Chinese people."

26. Marek   *From: Poland   Native Language: Polish*

"Taking Economics and Business, I was concerned it would be very difficult."

"College programs in Unites States are much different than in Poland. Students take fewer classes that are more focused around their field of study. In Poland there are still a lot of general knowledge courses as it was in High School."

27. Walid   *From: Algeria   Native Language: Arabic-French*

"I thought that it would be a great cross-cultural and academic experience. In terms of communication and socialization, I didn't think that it would be difficult for me as I was a young professional back home. In terms of language, my personal skills in English acquired over several years have enabled me to adapt very quickly to slang and also academic language, although I had some troubles with some new expressions and phrasal issues at the beginning, but overall, before coming to the U.S., I knew that in terms of language, it wouldn't be too difficult for me to speak and understand people. In terms of socializing, as I am naturally an outgoing person, very communicative and tolerant of cultural differences, I knew that it wouldn't be too difficult for me to make friends here in the U.S. I actually started making some friends online before coming to the U.S. Also I knew that my self-confidence and my strong personality would enable me to approach people, talk to them, and make friends."

"In terms of school, I didn't know a lot of things about the grading system here in the U.S.A., and the teaching methods. I knew that I would be facing a lot of challenges, but it was completely different from my preconceptions. The only real difference is about the American lifestyle, but I have found it very simple, not really complicated, and it was very easy for me to adapt. Maybe it's because I am used to traveling and can adapt to cultural differences. Also, I have always valued the U.S.A. and the American way of life, so I really don't think that my previous thoughts have changed a lot. However, my big surprise, is noticing how much Americans are very accepting and very friendly towards internationals. Wherever I've gone here in the U.S., people were just amazing to me, very friendly and very helpful."

28. Anastasia *From: Russia   Native Language: Russian*

"I thought I would need time to adjust to the language anyway. I was a little bit nervous. But I knew that the U.S. is a country of immigrants, so it did not bother me much."

"Many things were as expected. I had a language barrier and had to adjust. But mostly what I thought was a language barrier, in fact was adjusting to the system, professors, ways of teaching. Thus, I didn't have much of a language problem. The only thing that still persists is that I still don't understand some American jokes and do not feel safe playing with the language as natives do."

29. Pei-Shan *From: Taiwan   Native Language: Chinese*

"I thought American classmates would not want to talk to foreigners. Americans are used to speaking their opinions in class and they love group discussion."

"People are really nice and willing to provide help. Before, I thought Americans were arrogant. They're more active in class then I imagined, and the professors' expectations and teaching styles are different from what I was used to. American classmates study hard too."

30. Kristin *From: Norway   Native Language: Norwegian*

"I was really excited to move to the United States, but I was a little bit concerned about communicating in English and if it would prevent me from expressing myself the way I wanted. I was also concerned about giving academic presentations since that is not something I had practiced a lot."

"After I moved here, I learned that people around me are really helpful and open to teaching me how to express myself better. When it comes to doing presentations, taking a class for international students was really helpful and gave me an advantage. Presentations are now not as frightening as I thought they would be."

31. Gibrilla   *From: Sierra Leone   Native Language: Limba*

"I expected it to be smooth sailing as I grew up in an English speaking country and had served as a teacher of English in my country for a considerable number of years."

"Some of my experiences were contrary to my prior expectation as there were times when they made me feel I was incomprehensible. I had to make a conscious effort to communicate my views and opinions both in class and out in the street. There were times when their actions were meant to spite me and sap my confidence, but I succeeded most of the time in changing the wrong perceptions and impressions."

32. Hiba   *From: Morocco   Native Language: Arabic and French*

"I thought it would be hard and that people might be judgmental because of my accent. I figured the classrooms would be regular classrooms, where professors make the law and it's their way or the highway."

"People ended up being very receptive and interested in my origins! People made the effort to listen to me and help me out when needed!"

33. Hashintha   *From: Sri Lanka   Native Language: Sinhalese*

"As a student, I expected that I would have to speak in class and converse with the lecturer. This was a barrier I knew I had to overcome before I came to the United States. The educational setting in Sri Lanka is obviously different from the U.S., and the marked difference is that there are few discussions between the students and the professor during the lecture session."

"Initially, I found it difficult to speak up in class, but this has changed after my experiences of being in the classroom atmosphere in United States. The atmosphere is relaxed and that made it easier to speak and contribute to the discussions in class."

34. Heyi *From: China   Native Language: Chinese*

"Get closer to a different cultures and improve my language skills."

"There is always a communication gap. Sometimes I don't know how to start and continue a good conversation with native speakers. Sometimes it seems the native speakers are not willing to share their stories or not interested in the topic for our conversation."

35. Ahmed *From: Iraq   Native Language: Arabic*

"I thought it would be very tough and challenging. I felt confused about what will I do in a completely different culture."

"From the moment I arrived at my university, I knew it was going to be a very nice and rich experience. Now I have friends from all over the world. I am totally comfortable with everything."

36. Olga *From: Russia   Native Language: Russian*

"I was anticipating a very friendly classroom atmosphere, with lots of group activities and free discussion. I believed this style of teaching would facilitate new friendships."

"My anticipations as per classroom atmosphere were confirmed. However, easy discussions in class did not lead to easily formed friendships, as classmates turned out to be very busy people outside school. Nevertheless, the general studying atmosphere is always pleasant and relaxed, and classmates are very nice and open people."

37. Miklos   *From: Hungary   Native Language: Hungarian*

"I was afraid of the accent. I thought the speaking would be easier than the reading part. I overcomplicated the writing part."

"Usually it was easy to understand Americans. I had some difficulties to 'enter' into an ongoing conversation, especially with background noise. Writing was much more easy than I thought, although I do make a lot of mistakes."

38. Shan   *From: China   Native Language: Chinese*

"It will be a different teaching style. More discussion. Making friends would not be easy because language is still a problem."

"It is almost the same as my expectations."

39. Katharine   *From: Switzerland   Native Language: English/French*

"Did not expect to encounter any major difficulties."

"I did not expect the change in exam format (in France, Switzerland a typical high school exam is four hours long). I was thrown by the forty-five minute format and the tiny blue books. Same goes for dissertations that went from a dozen handwritten pages to 500 typed words."

40. Chen   *From: China   Native Language: Chinese*

"Everything would be in English and I would be carrying a dictionary around."

"I don't really need a dictionary because I can understand others through body language and other visual help."

41. Anis   *From: Algeria   Native Language: Arabic*

"I didn't think language would be an issue; in fact the only concern I had was the intensity of the classes as well as [adapting] to the new teaching style."

"It has changed in the way I communicate with my professors and classmates; i.e., less barriers compared to my university in Algeria."

42. Dario   *From: Portugal   Native Language: Portuguese*

"I was expecting some challenges as far as a language barrier, English in the U.S. is quite different from 'European' taught English."

"I would never guess that Boston would be such a 'European' city. People were nice and helpful. I was not expecting so warm a welcome and help from professors, American students, or even the population in general. So, the first weeks were hard, but then the ear got used to it and everything was easy."

43. Abdulrahman   *From: Saudi Arabia*
Native Language: Arabic

"I think first of all, you have to find a good school because it will help you to improve your language. Also, you should live with an American family to practice English with them."

"It's a good thing because you see a different life, food, and education."

44. Sara   *From: Taiwan   Native Language: Mandarin*

"I had been working on speaking fluently in English before I arrived [in the United States] and imagined that it would improve my oral communication. I did not perceive any communication problems because I had been told that my English was good. I understood that classes would be full of interaction and I prepared for this."

"Getting a high TOEFL score doesn't mean you are a good communicator. There are so many underlying nonverbal expressions in American culture and rules that you have to follow. Fluency in English can be improved by studying, but there are so many things you will never know if no one tells you."

45. Jordan   *From: France   Native Language: French*

"Unlimited resources, everyone is friendly, teaching style is dynamic involving the students in a conversation instead of just lecturing."

"What I have seen is that most Americans will hold a warm facade which can be very deceiving for internationals. In my county people are colder in the beginning but will after a while hold deeper and in my opinion a healthier and more meaningful relationship. From what I have been able to gather, the focus on furthering one's career and own individuality is so strong in America that it trumps over everything else, including relationships which leaves most feeling lonely even though they are surrounded by 'friends' and 'colleagues.' These friends are mostly contacts to further one's network. A story to illustrate this is how at a party, when holding a conversation, most will always be looking in the room for someone else (regardless of whom they are speaking to) for any new occasion to strengthen one's overall network."

46. Green   *From: South Korea   Native Language: Korean*

"Before I came to the United States, I didn't think there would be a huge difference between how I study and how students in the U.S. study. South Korea is place where students study day and night. There are rarely breaks and there is a lot of pressure from family, teachers, and classmates. I could not imagine that the U.S. would be different."

"I think education in the United States, and its style is very different from South Korea. It is really up to the students whether to choose to study or not. While students back in my country are usually forced or pressured to study, student in the U.S. are encouraged to study. There is much more freedom and more choices for students here and I really enjoy that privilege."

47. Yinfei *From: China   Native Language: Chinese*

"I thought it would be a little difficult for me because speaking in English was always a little scary for me. I also heard there would be lots of readings for us and studying was quite hard. I also learnt that people here were very active in class, which was quite different from us. And, teachers were demanding especially in class participation. But I thought American people were friendly and nice, so I thought I might be on good terms with them."

"I think professors here are willing to help and really care about problems in class. At first, it was a little intimidating to speak in class, and I really didn't know how I'd perform in class. But after a while, the situation became much better and professors would give some useful feedback and encouragement. Therefore, I think it is really nice and I have learnt a lot and am quite active in class now. The biggest change is being able to 'speak out.' Meanwhile, I have several foreign friends as well. But some of my classmates are not so interested in making friends with us. Maybe because we don't have much work experience and we don't share similar topics. I'm still trying to fit into the American ways of making friends. I was not so willing to go out to a party on weekends, but now it seems a good way to get to know each other. I will attend a friend's party occasionally now and try to get used to the American style of building networks."

48. Mirjam   *From: Germany   Native Language: German*

"Didn't expect any issues except problems with written language."

"My English is better than I expected, no real problems occurred."

49. Arwa   *From: India   Native Language: Gujarati and English*

"I am from India and my accent is Indian. I didn't change it because one, I wanted to be natural and secondly, I assumed that American people wouldn't find it hard to comprehend an Indian accent and I was partially right. They understood me for the most part, but there were a few instances in my life where I had trouble getting people to understand my accent and these instances were easy to catch as I made the same mistakes twice or thrice. There was a lot of confusion around words that had certain sounds. 'T' in America is pronounced like 'd.' I was embarrassed once at a grocery store because the helper clearly couldn't help me find what I was looking for in spite of repeated attempts at explaining it. He couldn't understand me when I used the word 'thermal.' I found comfort with the classroom teaching style very disconcerting. Once in class when one of my professors thought that English was my second language, I was confused if my English was all that bad. I knew my professor was not being mean though and yet I was offended. The thing is I went to a Catholic Convent (high school) back in India where the medium of instruction is British English. Spoken and written English is part of me. All my courses were in English, and I speak to my parents in English, not my mother tongue."

"I never made American friends, but I believe strongly in American open heartedness and open mindedness. American classmates understood my English, and I understood their English. So it was not the lack of understanding, but the lack of communication, really. My classmates and I never got enough opportunity, and since building relationships takes time, I felt two years was not enough for me to win the hearts of my classmates. I worked hard to maintain lasting friendships with two friends, but they didn't augur well. They didn't know when I left America. They didn't realize I was trying very hard to maintain a lasting relationship. They just didn't respond enough."

50. Valeria   *From: Columbia   Native Language: Spanish*

"My only knowledge of American schools came from Hollywood teenage comedies. I didn't know what to expect. I didn't know if people would judge me for my accent or my nationality."

"It turned out to be very different than what I expected. Especially in a city where there are students from all over the planet. Everyone is very understanding of international students."

References

1. FMI Food Marketing Institute, Washington D.C. 'Natural and Organic Foods' www.fda.gov/ohrms/dockets/dockets/06p0094/06p-0094-cp00001-05-Tab-04-Food-Marketing-Institute-vol1.pdf

2. Hall, E. T. 1959. The Silent Language. Garden City, NY: Doubleday.

EXCUSE ME, CAN YOU REPEAT THAT?

Order Form

ITEM	QTY	Unit Price	TOTAL
Excuse Me, Can You Repeat That?		$14.95	
ISBN: 978-1-58985-256-3		**Subtotal**	
* 8.8% sales tax – on all orders originating in Arizona.		***Tax**	
* $8.00 or 10% of the total order – whichever is greater. Ground shipping. Allow 1 to 2 weeks for delivery.		**Shipping**	
Mail form to: Five Star Publications, Inc. PO Box 6698, Chandler, AZ 85246-6698		**TOTAL**	

NAME:

ADDRESS:

CITY, STATE, ZIP:

DAYTIME PHONE: **FAX:**

EMAIL:

Method of Payment:
❏VISA ❏Master Card ❏Discover Card ❏American Express

account number   expiration date

signature   3-4 digit security number

❏ Yes, please send me a Five Star Publications catalog.
How were you referred to Five Star Publications?
❏ Friend ❏ Internet ❏ Book Show ❏ Other

Five Star Publications
A Resource for Every Author & Publisher Since 1985

P.O. Box 6698 • Chandler, AZ 85246-6698
(480) 940-8182   866-471-0777 Fax: (480) 940-8787
info@FiveStarPublications.com www.FiveStarPublications.com